A SHORT HIST

On cover: The Four Moors coat of arms of Sardinia

Cover illustration: Alberto Paba Associati
Graphic design, pagination, photo-litho: Editing CDE
English translation: David C. Nilson, DipTrans IoL, MIL

ISBN 88-7138-323-0

A Short History of Sardinia

by Francesco Cesare Casula

Carlo Delfino editore

Female statuette from
Cuccuru s'Arriu (Cabras).

Sardinian Prehistory

Sardinia is one of the oldest lands in Europe. There has been human presence since the Palaeolithic, but the first permanent settlements were established much later, in the Neolithic, some time around 6000 BC.

AGE		SARDINIAN CULTURES AND CIVILIZATIONS	CHRONOLOGY
PALAEOLITHIC	LOWER	CLACTONIAN; RÍO ALTANA (Perfugas)	2000000; 450000; 150000; 100000
	MIDDLE	NO FINDINGS	35000
	UPPER	GROTTA CORBEDDU (Oliena)	
MESOLITHIC			1000
NEOLITHIC	EARLY	IMPRESSED POTTERY TRADINIG IN OBSIDIAN	6000
	MIDDLE	BONUIGHINU	4000
	LATE	SAN MICHELE	3240; 2700
AENEOLITHIC OR COPPER AGE		FILIGOSA; ABEALZU; MONTE CLARO; BELL BEAKERS	1800
BRONZE		BONNANARO; NURAGIC CIVILIZATION	1500
		COMBED POTTERY AND MYCENAEAN IMPORTS	1300; 850
IRON		GEOMETRIC POTTERY BRONZE STATUETTES STATUES; PHOENICIANS	750
HISTORICAL		POTTERY LATE NURAGIC; PUNIC CIVILIZATION	535; 238 B.C.
		ROMAN CIVILIZATION	476 A.D.

The first humans to settle in Gallura and northern Sardinia probably arrived from the Italian peninsula, and in particular from Etruria. It is thought that those who populated the central area of the island around the lagoons of Cabras and Santa Giusta came from the Iberian peninsula, passing through the Balearic Islands. Those who created

The Settling of Sardinia in prehistory.

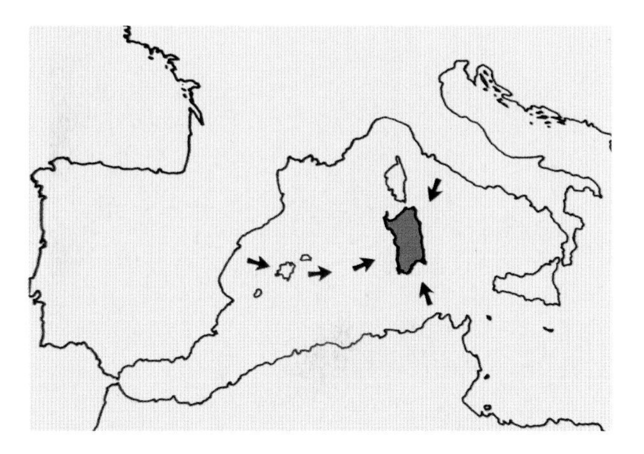

the settlements around the Gulf of Cagliari in the south were probably from Africa. Later on, there came groups from Anatolia and the Aegean Sea. Thus it can be said that Sardinia has never had a single population but several different ones.

With the passing of time the Sardinian peoples

Flat female statuette in fretworked marble.

Prehistoric arrowheads (Archaeological Museum in Cagliari).

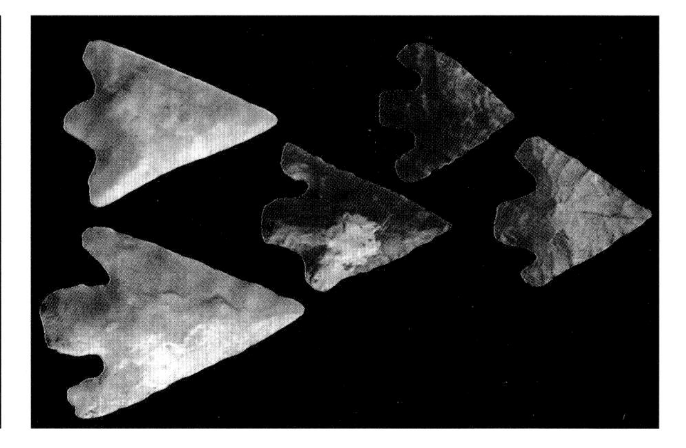

Copper Age pottery (Archaeological Museum in Sassari).

became culturally amalgamated in language and customs, but remained politically divided into small tribes, sometimes united in confederations, sometimes divided by war among themselves.
The tribes lived in villages of circular stone huts with straw roofs, similar to today's shepherd's *pinnetta*.

A shepherds's "pinnetta" today.

Starting from about 1500 BC, the villages were built at the foot of imposing fortresses in the form of a truncated cone (often reinforced and extended with the addition of secondary towers around the main one). These were given the name of *nuraghe*. Tribal boundaries were protected by small

The nuragic village at Barumini (Province of Cagliari).

nuraghi erected in strategic positions serving as watchtowers against surprise raids. Today, there are some seven thousand nuraghi in Sardinia.

Watchtower nuraghe.

Sardinia's ancient history

Around the year 1000 BC, the Phoenicians began arriving more and more often along Sardinia's coasts. They were traders who came from Lebanon and reached as far as Britain. Thus they needed landing places at night and in stormy weather.

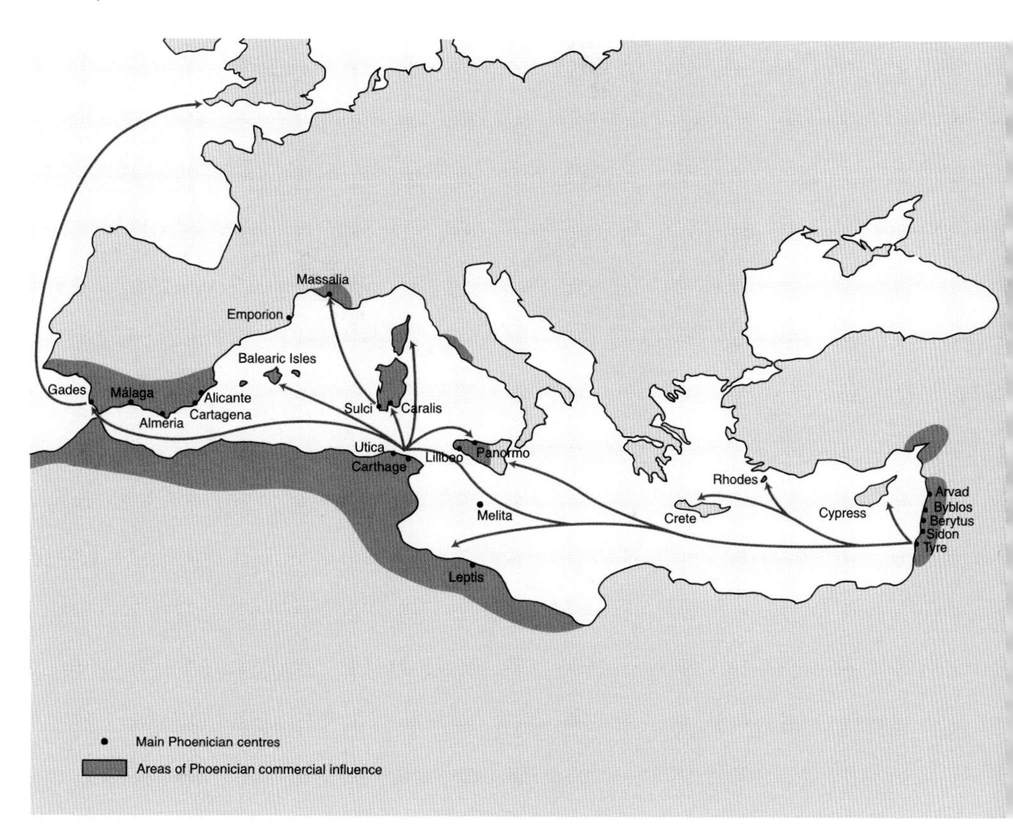

Phoenician landing places and routes in the Mediterranean to Britain.

With the permission of the local tribal chiefs, the most frequented landing places were those which later assumed the names of Caralis, Nora, Bithia, Sulci, Tharros, Bosa, Torres and Olbia, which quite soon became important trading centres and then true towns inhabited by Phoenician families who traded on the seas and with the nuragic Sardinians of the interior.

Phoenician ship.

In 509 BC, since Phoenician penetration into the interior was becoming deeper and more threatening, the Sardinians attacked the coastal towns inhabited by foreigners, who asked Carthage for help in defending themselves.

Nuragic warriors.

Necklace with vitreous paste beads and scarabs traded by the Phoenicians.

Main Phoenician trading centres.

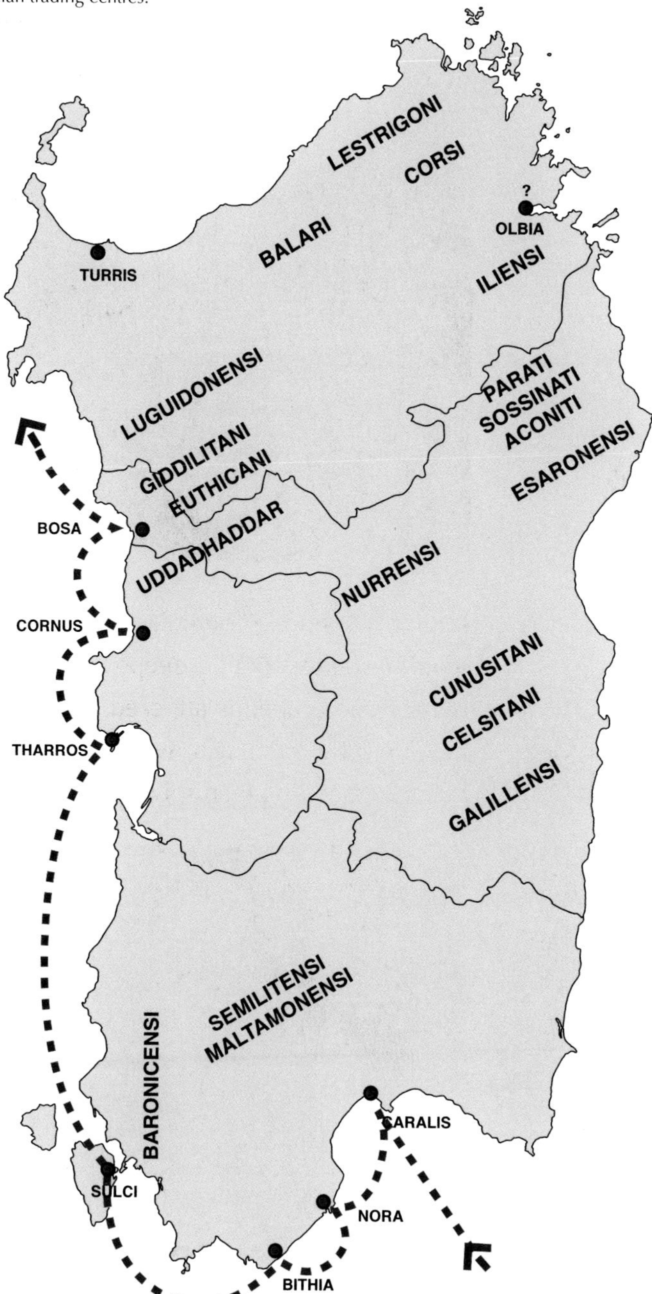

Maximum expansion of the Carthaginian Empire.

In several military campaigns, the Carthaginians, or Punic peoples, defeated the Sardinians and took possession of the entire island except for the mountainous part, later to be called *Barbària* or *Barbagia.*

The nuragic civilization: large sandstone head of a warrior.

Punic civilization: female divinity.

Punic expansion.

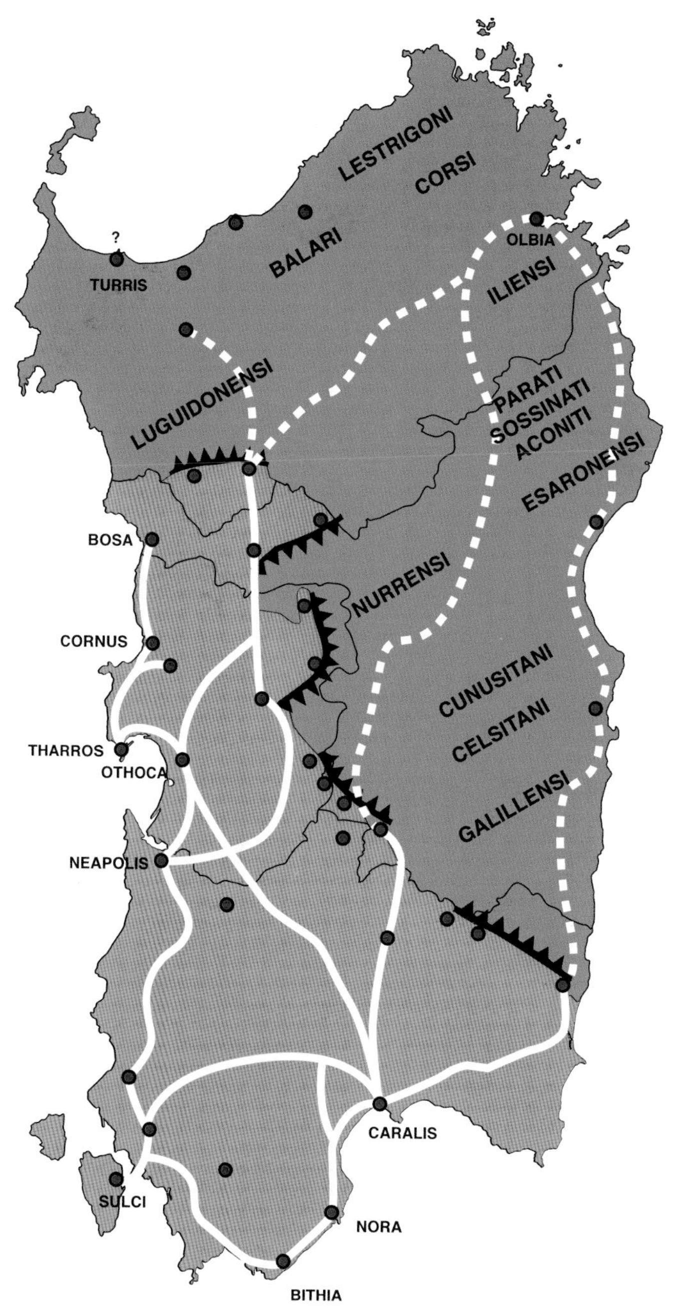

For two hundred and seventy-one years the splendid Carthaginian, or Punic, civilization remained in close contact with the fascinating indigenous nuragic civilization.

Following their defeat at the hands of the Romans in the First Punic War in 238 BC, the

Senatorial and imperial provinces.

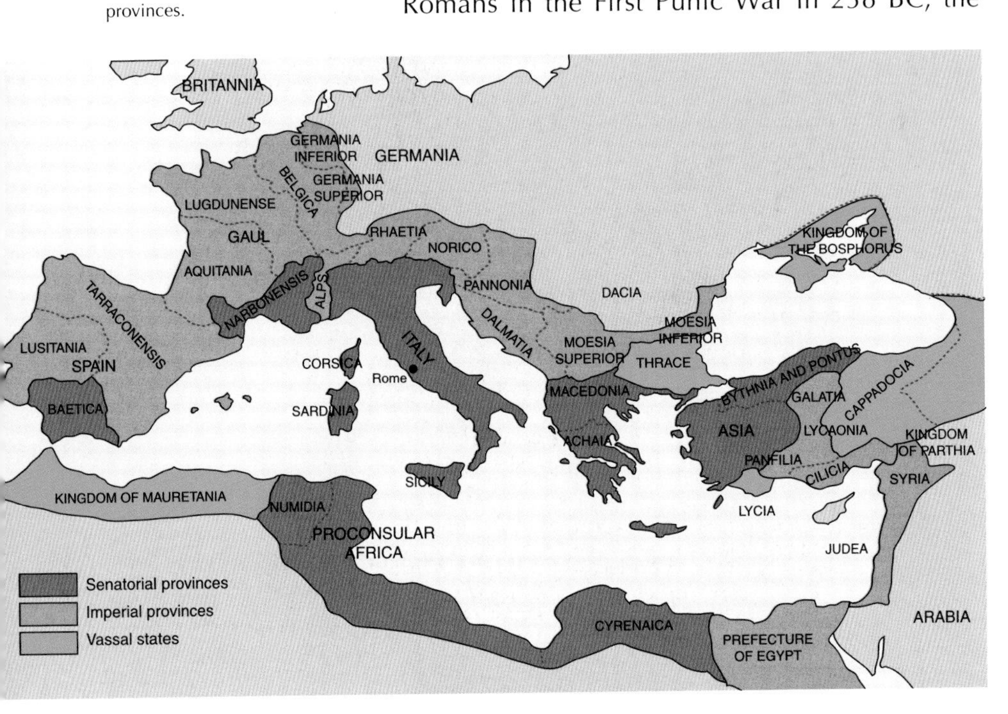

Ostia: Mosaic of a Roman ship at Turris (Porto Torres).

Main Roman roads.

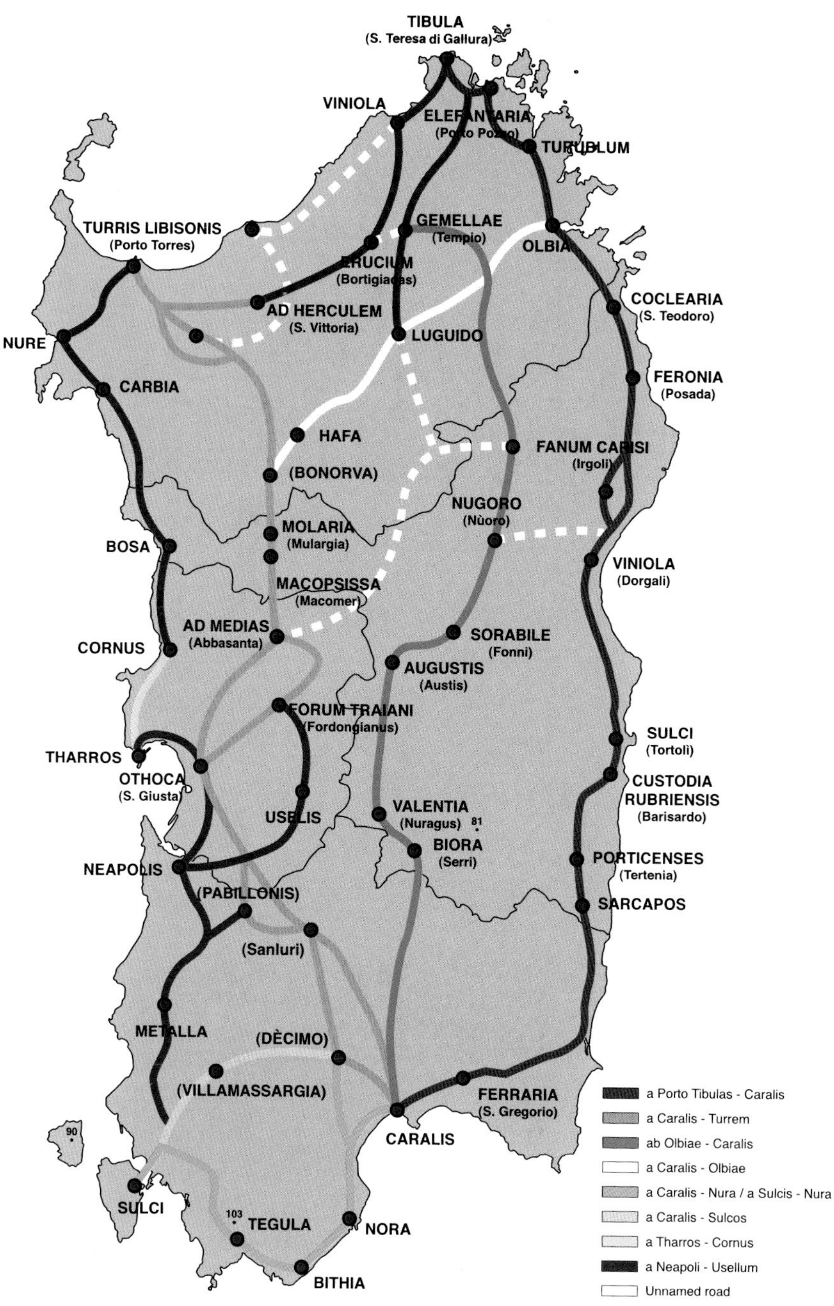

Ruins of the Punic-Roman town of Tharros (Oristano).

Carthaginians ceded Sardinia, which became a Roman province.

The Romans expanded and embellished the coastal towns and penetrated militarily even into Barbagia, thus bringing the nuragic civilization to an end.

Rome's domination of Sardinia lasted six hundred and ninety-four years. The Sardinians who inhabited the mountains often fought against the

Roman milestone.

Roman coin in honour of the Sardinian divinity Sardus Pater Babai.

Evolution of the Sardinian language over the centuries.

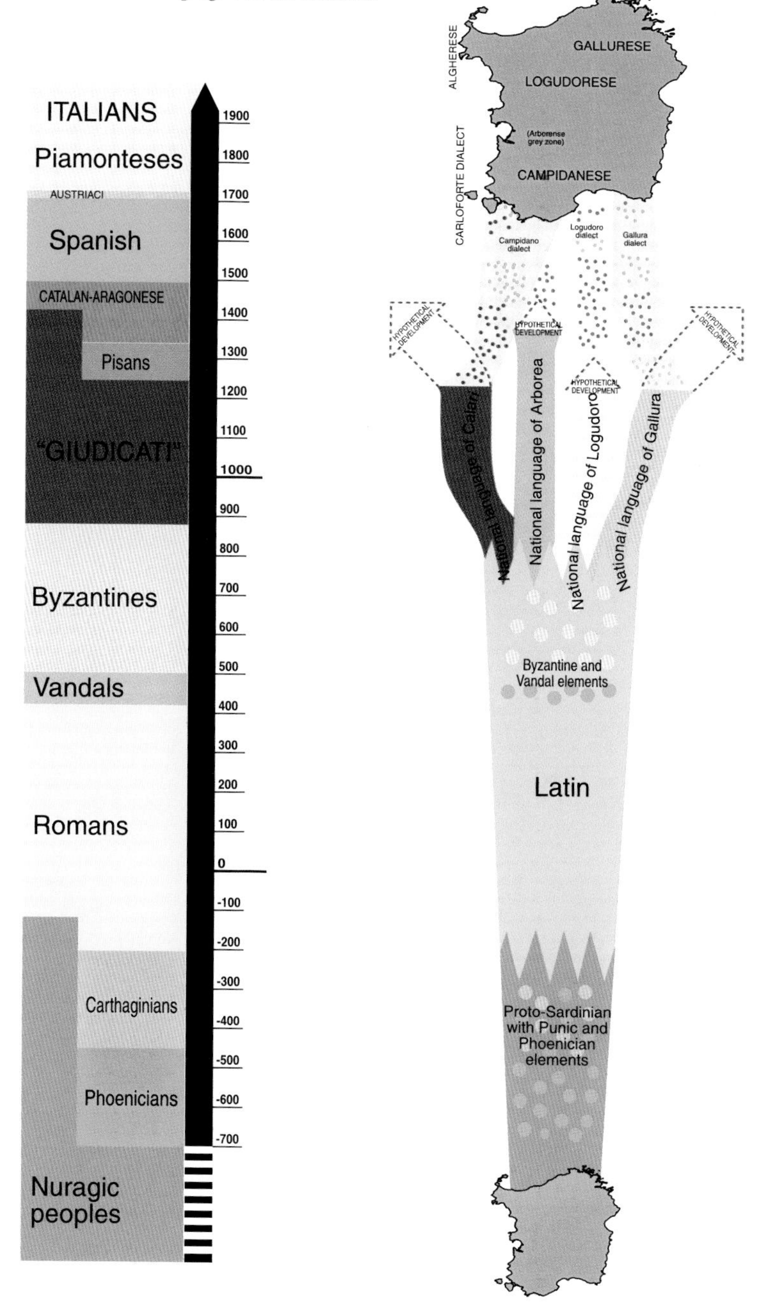

The Roman defensive lines against the peoples of the Barbagia regions.

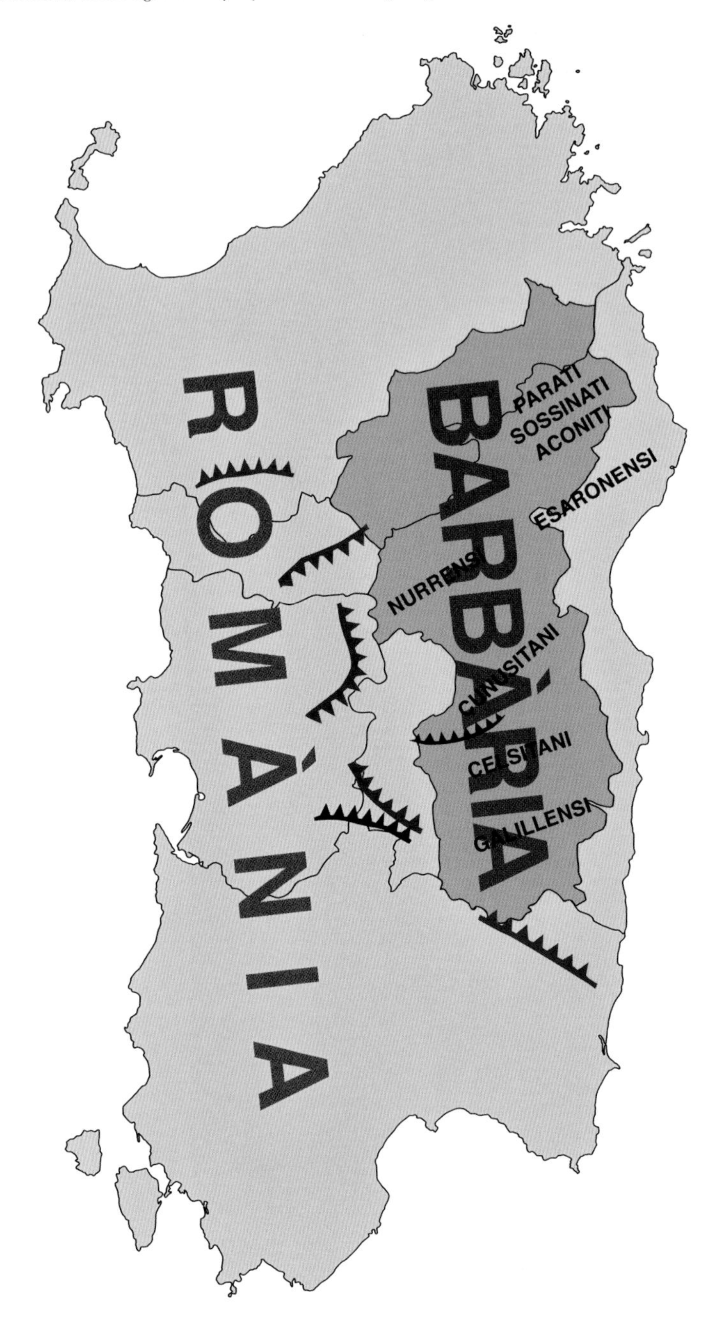

Romans, but in the end they adopted their language and civilization.

In 456 AD, when the Roman Empire was prostrated by decadence, the Vandals from Africa, on their return from a raid in Latium, occupied

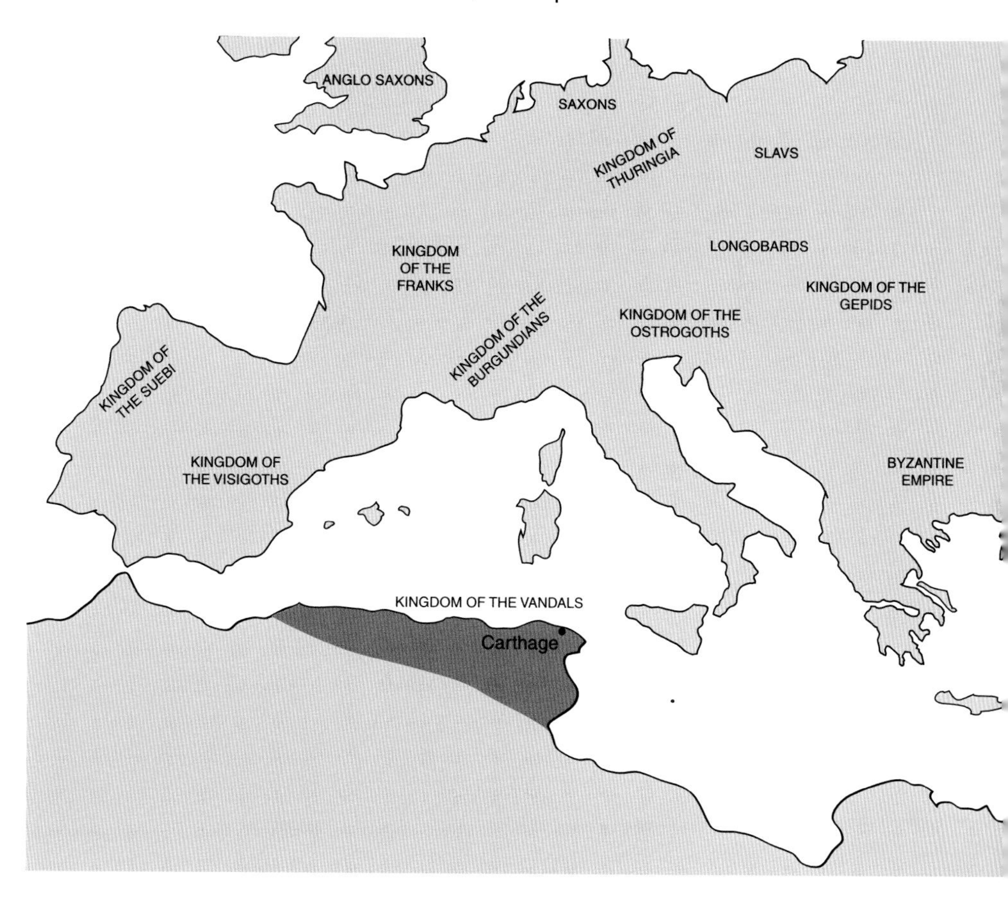

Caralis and the other coastal towns of Sardinia.

The Vandal Empire.

In 534 the Vandals were defeated at Tricamari – a place thirty kilometres from Carthage – by the troops of the Byzantine Emperor Justinian, and Sardinia became Byzantine.

The island was divided into districts called *merèie* governed by a *judex* whose seat was Caralis (Cagliari). The districts were presided over by an army stationed at Forum Traiani (today's Fordongianus) under the command of a *dux*.

A Byzantine inscription in Porto Torres (Province of Sassari).

With the Byzantines and the eastern monasticism of the Basilians, Christianity spread throughout the island, except in the Barbagia regions where, at the end of the 6th century, a short-lived independent state was created with Sardinian-pagan religious traditions, one of the kings of which was Ospitone.

A Sardinian-Byzantine Cross.

Pagan idols at Goni (Province of Cagliari).

From 640 to 732 the Arabs occupied North Africa, Spain and a part of France. In 827 they began their occupation of Sicily. Sardinia remained isolated and had to see to its own defence.

Arab expansion and incursions in Sardinia.

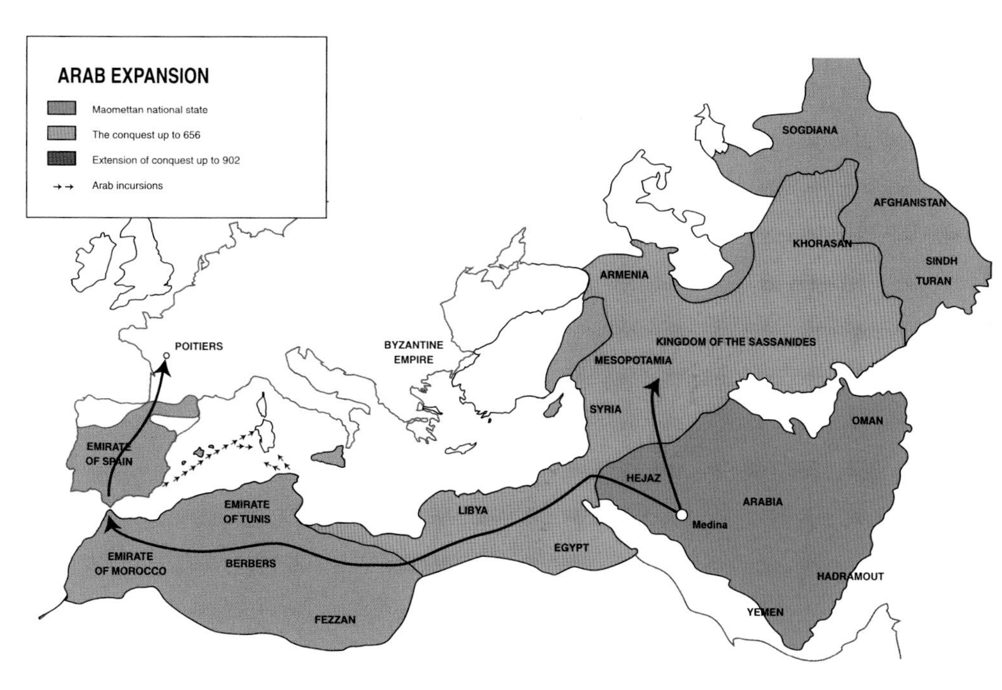

Thus the *judex Provinciae* became a single supreme head, with civil and military powers.

Because of the continuous raids and attacks along the Sardinian coasts by the Berbers converted to Islam, which began in 703 and became more and more ferocious as time went by, the coastal towns and villages were gradually abandoned by the inhabitants. The *judex Provinciae,* better to defend the island, delegated his civil and military powers to four of his deputies in the *merèie* of Calari, Torres, Gallura and Arborèa who, some time around the year 900, gained independence and became *judices* (in Sardinian *judikes* = kings) in their own right in their *Logu*, or state.

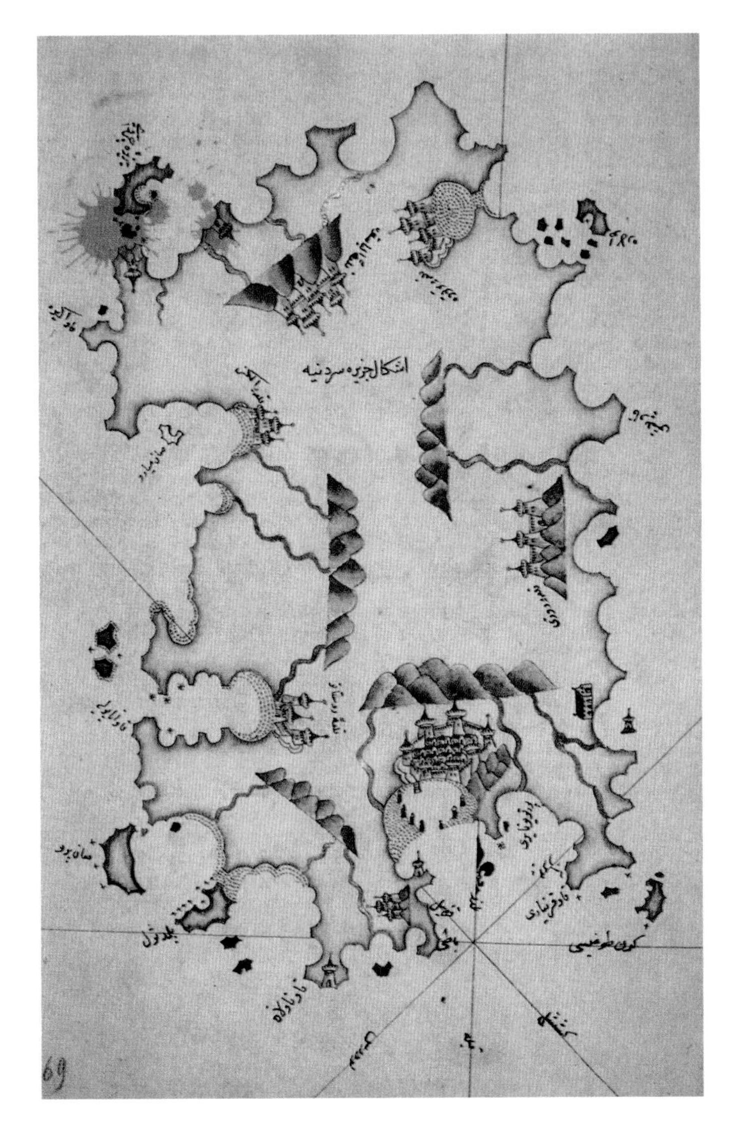

Sardinia as seen by an Arab cartographer.

The kingdoms of Càlari, Torres, Gallura and Arborèa.

Sardinia's medieval history

Each of these four Sardinian states – commonly referred to as *"giudicati"* – was a sovereign entity, not patrimonial but supra-individual in that it was not the property of the monarch, and democratic in that all the most important decisions were not made by the king (or "judike") but by the representatives of the people in a parliament called the *Corona de Logu*.

Each kingdom had its own boundaries with cas-

A lead seal of Barisone I, King of Torres.

Stone effigy of the sovereigns of Arborea Mariano IV and Ugone III at San Gavino Monreale (Province of Cagliari).

tles in defence of its political and commercial interests, its own parliament, its own laws (*Cartas de Logu*), its own national languages, its own

The Castle of Goceano with the town (today Burgos) at its foot.

public administrations, coats of arms and symbols.

Politically, the kingdom or "giudicato" of Calari sided with the Genoese. It came to an end in 1258 when its capital, Santa Igia, was attacked and destroyed by a coalition of Sardinian and Pisan forces. Its territory thus became a colony of the Republic of Pisa.

The kingdom or "giudicato" of Torres was instead

Ruins of Sant'Igia, capital of the Kingdom or "Giudicato" of Calari.

pro-Pisan and came to an end effectively in 1259 with the death of Queen Adelasia and officially in 1272 with the death of King Enzo.

The land was divided among the Ligurian Doria

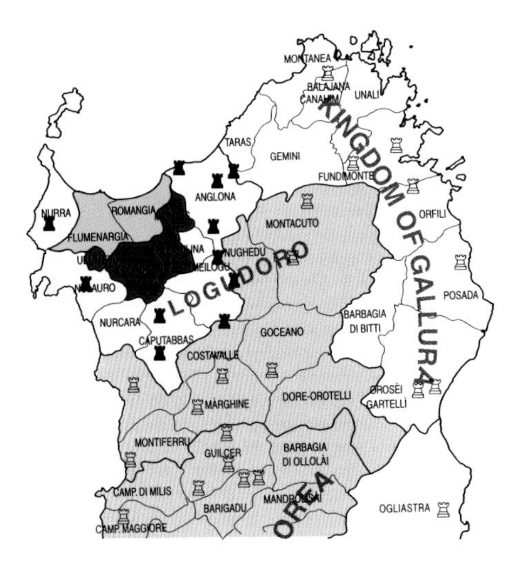

Division of the Kingdom of Torres between the kings of Arborea and the Sardinian Doria family.

Parchment of Enzo, King of Torres (State Archives of Macerata).

family and the indigenous Bas-Serra family that ruled in Arborea, while the town of Sassari with its lands set itself up as a republican state of the municipal kind.

The kingdom or "giudicato" of Gallura came to

Sassari's ancient city walls.

Dante Alighieri and Nino Visconti, "*judike*" of Gallura in a 14th-century miniature.

an end in 1288 when the last sovereign, Nino Visconti, a friend of Dante's, was exiled by the Pisans, who occupied the land.

The kingdom or "giudicato" of Arborea was almost always under the political and cultural influence of the powerful Republic of Pisa. It lasted some five hundred and twenty years, with Oristano as its capital.

Oristano. Buildings belonging to the royal palace, with Port'a Mari and the tower of San Filippo prior to its demolition in a drawing made in 1862.

Oristano. Tower of Mariano II of Arborea and Port'a Pontis.

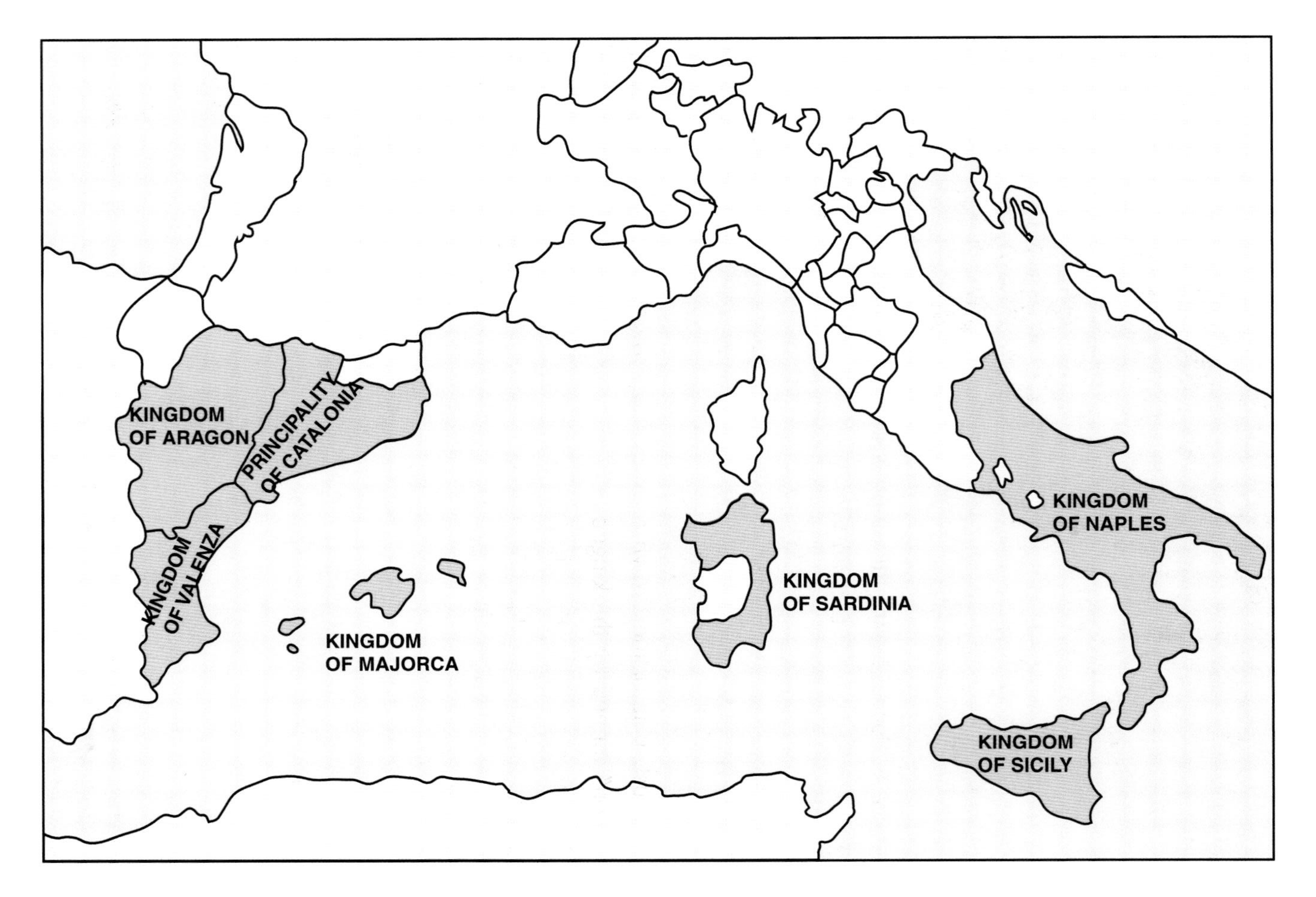
KINGDOM OF ARAGON
PRINCIPALITY OF CATALONIA
KINGDOM OF VALENZA
KINGDOM OF MAJORCA
KINGDOM OF SARDINIA
KINGDOM OF NAPLES
KINGDOM OF SICILY

Old Saint Peter's in Rome.

In 1297, Pope Boniface VIII, in order to bring to a negotiated end the Sicilian Vespers, which had broken out in 1282 between the Angevins and the Aragonese for possession of Sicily, created *motu proprio* a virtual *regnum Sardiniae et Corsicae* and entrusted it to the Catalan James II the Just, king of the Crown of Aragon (a "royal union" formed by the kingdoms of Aragon and Valencia plus the Principality of Catalonia), promising him his support should he decide to conquer Pisan Sardinia in exchange for Sicily.

Facing page:
Mediterranean expansion of the Crown of Aragon from James II (1324) to Alfonso V (1443).

James II of Aragon in a miniature in the *Llibre Verd de Lleida.*

Coat of arms of the house of the Counts of Barcelona, sovereigns of Aragon.

Sardinia's modern history

In 1323, James II of Aragon formed an alliance with the sovereigns of Arborea and, following a military campaign lasting about one year, on 19 June 1324 conquered the Pisan lands of Cagliari and Gallura as well as the town of Sassari, and constituted a sovereign but imperfect state with the title and name of "Kingdom of Sardinia and Corsica".

Dynasty of the counts-kings of Barcelona in a 15th-century plate.

This kingdom was immediately brought under the Crown of Aragon and administered by a deputy of the king, first called the governor general and later viceroy. The towns of Cagliari, Iglesias and Sassari paid their tributes directly to the sovereign and for this reason were called

The Kingdom of Arborea and the Kingdom of Sardinia.

"royal towns"; the villages were grouped into fiefs and paid taxes to the feudal baron.
In 1353, for reasons of state survival, war broke out between the Kingdom of Arborea, which wanted to unite the whole island under its aegis, and the Kingdom of Sardinia and Corsica.

Aerial view of Alghero.

In 1354 the Aragonese captured Alghero and turned it into a totally Catalan town, which still today conserves its Iberian origins.
In 1355, Peter IV of Aragon, called the

Ceremonious, set up a parliament with powers to propose legislation in the "Kingdom of Sardinia and Corsica". The judiciary was represented by the Royal Council of Justice which in 1504 was transformed into the Royal Audience.

Coat of arms of the Kingdom or "Giudicato" of Arborea.

From 1365 to 1409, the kings or "judikes" of Arborea Mariano IV, Ugone III, Mariano V (aided by his mother Eleonora, the famous queen-regent) and Guglielmo III (the French nephew of Eleonora) succeeded in occupying almost the entire island except for Castel di Cagliari (today's Cagliari) and Alghero.

Tomb of Martin the Young in the Cathedral of Cagliari.

In 1409, Martin the Young, king of Sicily and heir to the throne of Aragon, defeated the Sardinians of the *judikes* and completed the con-

Map of the Kingdom of Arborea
from 1365 to 1409.

quest of Sardinia in its entirety; shortly thereafter he died of malaria in Cagliari, leaving no legitimate heirs and the Crown of Aragon passed into the hands of the Castilian Trastámara dynasty, in the person of Fernando I of Antequera and his descendents – with the Compromise of Caspe in 1412.

In 1479, following the personal union between Ferdinand II of Aragon and Isabella of Castilia (called the *Catholic Sovereigns*) who had married ten years before, the Crown of Spain came into being.

Coat of arms of the Kingdom of Sardinia.

The Kingdom of Sardinia (which in the new name was separated from Corsica since that island had never been conquered) also became

Spanish, with the coat of arms of the Four Moors. Following the failure of his anti-Muslim military campaigns in Tunis (1535) and Algiers (1541), Charles I (or V) of Spain ordered the building of a series of coastal watchtowers along Sardinia's coasts to defend his Mediterranean possessions against raids by Barbary pirates from Africa.

The Kingdom of Sardinia remained a Spanish possession for some four hundred years, from 1324 to 1720, absorbing many Spanish traditions, customs, linguistic expressions and lifestyles, today represented by the traditional processions of Sant'Efisio in Cagliari (1 May) the Cavalcade in Sassari (next-to-last Sunday in May) and the Redeemer in Nuoro (29 August).

The watchtower against raids by Barbary pirates at Cala d'Ostia (Pula).

Feast of Sant'Efisio in Cagliari.

In 1708, in the course of the War of the Spanish Succession, which saw Philip of Bourbon pitted against Charles of Hapsburg, the government of the Kingdom of Sardinia passed effectively into

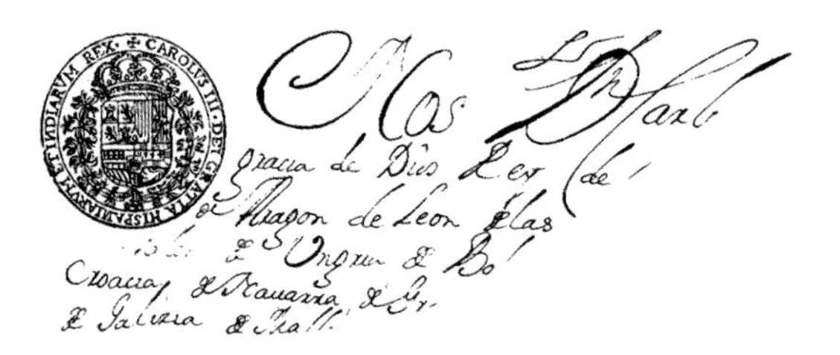

Document with seal of Charles III (or IV) of Austria.

the hands of the Hispano-Austrians who had invaded the island.

Oil painting of Philip V of Spain.

Solemn deed with boxed pendant seal issued in 1722 by Victor Amedeus II of Savoy, former king of Sardinia.

In 1717, Cardinal Alberoni, minister of Philip V of Spain, reoccupied the island.
In 1718, with the Treaty of London, the Kingdom of Sardinia was ceded to the dukes of Savoy, the princes of Piedmont, who incorporated it federally into their continental possessions. The

Insular and continental lands of the Kingdom of Sardinia prior to the unification of Italy
(from *La Terra*, published by De Agostini).

Kingdom became Italian.

In 1799, due to the Napoleonic wars in Italy, the Savoys left Turin and took refuge in Cagliari, capital of the Kingdom, for about fifteen years.

Tomb of Charles Emmanuel of Savoy in the crypt of the Cathedral in Cagliari.

The royal palace in Cagliari up to the "merger" in 1847.

In 1847 the Sardinians spontaneously gave up their status as an independent state and "merged" with Piedmont to have a single parliament, a single judiciary and a single government in Turin. The unified Kingdom of Sardinia was perfected with the *summa potestas,* which is to say the faculty of directly stipulating international treaties.

Throne of the Kingdom of Sardinia in the royal palace in Turin.

Painting of the *Risorgimento.*

The year 1848 saw the beginning of the wars of independence for the unity of the Italian peninsula conducted by the king of Sardinia for thirteen years.

On 17 March 1861 the Kingdom of Sardinia changed its name to that of Kingdom of Italy.

The Italian flag on the turret of the Quirinale, now residence of the Italian president of the republic.

Sardinia's contemporary history

In 1946, following a referendum, the Kingdom of Italy became the Republic of Italy. Sardinia, which since 1948 has been governed with a special statute, today has 1,628,690 inhabitants in the four provinces of Cagliari, Sassari, Oristano and Nuoro, which are more or less the same as the lands of the four ancient and glorious states of the *judikes*.

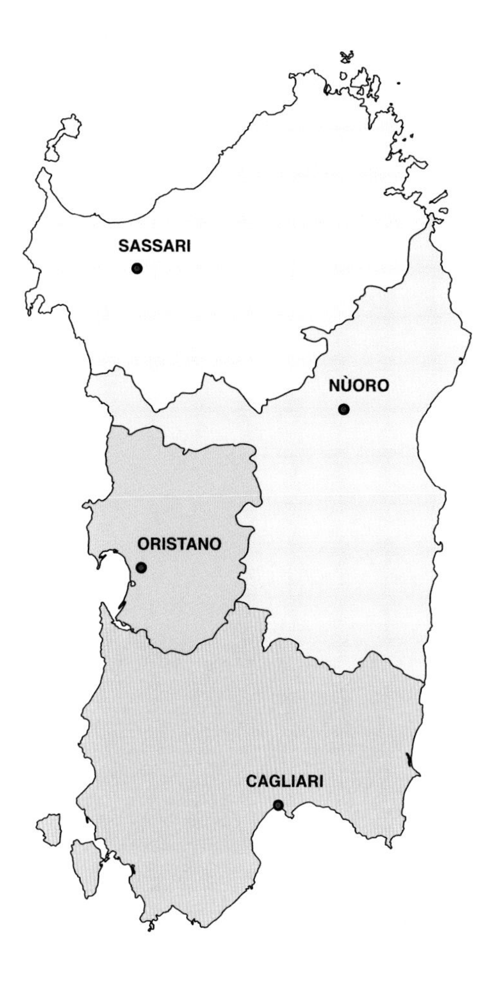

Sardinia today with its four provinces.

Contents

Sardinian Prehistory

Sardinia's ancient history

Sardinia's medieval history

Sardinia's modern history

Sardinia's contemporary history

Printed in July 2004
by Litograf Editor s.r.l., Città di Castello